D1579689

MACMILL
PRE-INTERM

DANIEL DEFOE

Robinson Crusoe

Retold by Salma Gabol

MACMILLAN

MACMILLAN READERS

PRE-INTERMEDIATE LEVEL

Founding Editor: John Milne

The Macmillan Readers provide a choice of enjoyable reading materials for learners of English. The series is published at six levels – Starter, Beginner, Elementary, Pre-intermediate, Intermediate and Upper.

Level Control
Information, structure and vocabulary are controlled to suit the students' ability at each level.

The number of words at each level:

Starter	about 300 basic words
Beginner	about 600 basic words
Elementary	about 1100 basic words
Pre-intermediate	about 1400 basic words
Intermediate	about 1600 basic words
Upper	about 2200 basic words

Vocabulary
Some difficult words and phrases in this book are important for understanding the story. Some of these words are explained in the story, some are shown in the pictures, and others are marked with a number like this: ...³. Words with a number are explained in the *Glossary* at the end of the book.

Answer Keys
Answer Keys for the *Points for Understanding* and *Exercises* sections can be found at www.macmillanenglish.com/readers.

Contents

A Note About The Author

Daniel Defoe was born in London in 1660. His father, James Foe, was a tallow chandler – he made candles[1] from animal fat. As a boy, Daniel Defoe lived through several very important events in history. When he was very young, London was hit by the plague, a terrible disease which killed many people. Soon after, the Great Fire of London burned down many of the houses near Defoe's family home.

Daniel Defoe had an interesting life. He went to school in Dorking and then trained to be a minister of the church – a religious[2] leader. However, he did not become a minister. Instead he worked as a merchant, travelling to many countries buying and selling things. He enjoyed going to other places, and was interested in travel throughout his life.

In 1684, Defoe married Mary Tuffley, with whom he had six children. He hoped to become a rich man, but he spent much of his life owing money to people.

In 1685, Defoe joined with a group of people, led by the Duke of Monmouth. These people wanted to get rid of[3] King James II. They fought against the King's soldiers and lost. Many of them were killed or sent away from England, but Defoe was forgiven[4]. However, in 1692 he was sent to prison because he owed a lot of money and could not pay it back.

Defoe started writing in 1697. He wrote short books and pieces for journals – magazines – about many things. Often he wrote about politics and the King. In 1703, he was sent to prison once more for his political writings, and after this he worked as a spy[5] for the government.

Defoe started writing novels when he was sixty years old. *Robinson Crusoe*, which was published in 1719, was very successful, and in 1722 he wrote *Moll Flanders*. Defoe died in 1731 and is buried[6] in Bunhill Fields in London.

A Note About This Story

Many people think of *Robinson Crusoe* as the first English novel. It became very popular as soon as it was published in April 1719, and has been well-loved ever since. It has been translated into many different languages and retold in many different ways over the years, for example in films and children's books.

Robinson Crusoe tells the story of an Englishman who spends twenty-eight years on an island near Venezuela, in Central America. Daniel Defoe may have got the idea for the novel from a true story about a man called Alexander Selkirk, who spent several years on an island called *Más a Tierra* in the Pacific. However, there were several other stories about people living on desert islands at this time. Defoe may have read or heard about these people, and they may have given him his ideas.

The island in the novel is probably meant to be the island of Tobago, near Trinidad in the Caribbean. At this time, many European countries such as Spain, Portugal, France and Britain had started to send people all over the world, buying and selling things and taking colonies – groups of people – which they treated as their own. When colonies were taken, the people who lived there were often treated very badly. In America and the Caribbean islands, the Europeans set up[7] big plantations[8], where they grew sugar and tobacco[9]. They needed people to work on their plantations, so they bought slaves[10] who were taken from Africa by ship.

In *Robinson Crusoe*, Crusoe sets up a sugar plantation in Brazil and then travels to Africa to buy slaves. His ship is wrecked[11] and he finds himself alone on a small island. The novel is about his adventures. But it is also about learning about yourself and making mistakes. It also shows Daniel Defoe's strong religious beliefs.

The Places in This Story

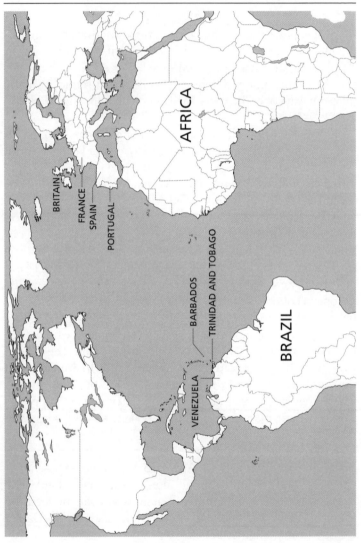

1

I Go to Sea

My name is Robinson Crusoe. I was born in 1632 in the city of York, in England. I came from a good family. My father was from Germany. He made his money as a merchant – buying and selling things – and came to live in York, where he married my mother.

I had two older brothers. One became a soldier and was killed in France. And I never knew what happened to my other brother – just as my mother and father never knew what happened to me.

I had a good education. I went to a good school, and learned a lot at home. My father wanted me to get a good job. But I had other ideas. I wanted to go to sea. I could not think about anything else, even though my parents and friends argued strongly against it. It was as if something was pushing me towards the terrible life that lay ahead of me. One day my father called me to his room and asked me why I wanted to leave his house, and England.

'People who go to sea are not like you,' he said. 'They either go because they have no money, or because they are very rich, and they want an adventure. You are lucky because you are neither rich nor poor. Poor people have to worry about finding food and somewhere to live. Rich people have to worry about looking after their money. You are in the best place, because you are in the middle. You can have a comfortable life if you stay at home.'

My father promised to do many things for me if I listened to him. With tears running down his face, he told me to remember my older brother. He had gone away to become a soldier and been killed.

'If you go to sea, God will not be pleased with you,' he warned me. 'I think you will be very sorry if you do not listen to me – and you will have no one to help you.'

I listened carefully to my father's words, and for a few days, I changed my mind about leaving home. But within a few weeks, I had decided to go away once more. I asked my mother to talk to my father. I told her that I wanted to go on one voyage[12]. I said that if I did not like it, I would come home and work very hard.

But my mother was very upset. She said she would not talk to my father. She said she did not know how I could even think of going to sea. And she told me that she would not help me to do foolish things with my life. A year went by, and my parents would still not let me go to sea.

Then one day I went to the city of Hull and met a friend. His father owned a ship which was sailing to London, and I decided to go with them, without even telling my mother or father.

When the ship left Hull, the wind began to blow and the sea turned rough[13]. As I had never been to sea before, I was terrified, and became very seasick[14]. Suddenly I thought about what I had done. I remembered my mother and father's words, and felt terribly sorry for not listening to them. I promised to myself that if God let me live, I would go straight home to my father and never go in a ship again.

The next day, the sea was a little calmer[15], but I still felt seasick. The following morning, however, when I got up, the sun was shining on a clear sea. I thought it was the most beautiful thing I had ever seen. That evening, I drank too much rum[16] with the other men on the ship. I completely forgot all the promises I had made when I felt so ill.

A few days later, when we came near the shore[17], a terrible storm blew up. The sea was very rough, and waves[18] that were as high as mountains broke over the ship every few minutes.

This storm was nothing like the first one. Even the other men on the ship had faces full of fear[19]. They said they had never seen anything like it. We all prayed[20] for our lives.

In the middle of the night, one of the men told us that there was a leak[21] in the ship – water was coming in. The men worked as hard as they could to get the water out, but everyone knew that the ship was going to sink[22]. I felt as if my heart had died inside me. The captain[23] told the men to fire[24] guns to show other boats that we needed help. But the sea was too rough for a boat to come near.

At last, however, the storm started to die down[25] a little, and a boat managed to come close to the ship. After trying many times, we finally pulled the boat near to our ship and climbed into it. As we rowed[26] away, we saw our ship go down in the rough sea. I was so frightened I almost couldn't watch.

We rowed safely to the shore, where we were well looked after. There, we were given enough money to go on to London or back to Hull. I could have gone back home to Hull. My father would have been pleased to see me, and I could have had a quiet happy life. But something inside me would not let me go back.

A few days later, I met my friend, whose father was the captain of the ship. My friend explained to his father that I had come on the voyage to see whether I would like to travel abroad by sea.

'Young man,' he said, 'you should never go to sea again. God is showing you what will happen if you ever go on another voyage.'

The captain asked me about myself. When I told him that my father had not wanted me to go to sea, he became quite angry.

'Why did this boy have to come into my ship?' he cried. 'Believe me, young man, if you do not go back home, terrible things will happen to you. Your father told you that God would not be pleased with you, and his words will come true.'

2

I Am Captured by Pirates[27]

I went to London, and stayed there for a while. I tried to decide whether to go home or go to sea. There I met the captain of a ship which was going to Africa. The captain was a very good man, and he said I could go with him. He told me to bring some toys and other small things to sell for gold. The voyage went very well, and when we came back, I sold the gold for a lot of money. This made me think that I could become very rich as a merchant.

My friend the captain taught me many things on that trip. I learnt all about sailing from him. But sadly he died soon after the voyage. The ship had a new captain now, and was going to Africa again. I decided to go on it once more. I asked the captain's widow[28] to look after some of my money, and I took the rest with me.

My second voyage to Africa did not go well. Early one morning, just off the coast of North Africa, a pirate ship began following us. We sailed away across the sea as fast as we could, but the ship kept following us. By the afternoon the pirates were very close. We fired our guns at them, but there were nearly two hundred of them. They came onto our ship, cutting down our sails[29] and killing three of our men. Several other men were hurt, and as the ship could no longer sail, we were captured by the pirates.

They took us to a place called Sallee, which was owned by Moors, people from north-west Africa. The other men from our boat were taken away, but I was kept in Sallee as the pirate captain's slave. I could not believe what had happened to me. I thought about my bad luck and I remembered my father's words. He had told me that if I went to sea I would be unhappy. He said that I would have no one to help me. And it seemed that he had been right. I did not know then that this was just the first of the many terrible things that would happen to me.

I worked as the pirate captain's slave for two years, and was always thinking of how I could escape. Then, one day, something happened which made me feel I might be able to get away. Once or twice a week, the pirate captain used to take me fishing with a slave boy called Xury in a little rowing boat. I was very good at catching fish and he sometimes used to send me out with Xury and one of his relatives, a man called Moley. One morning, when we went out fishing, a thick fog came up. We could not see the shore. We rowed all day and the next night, and when morning came, we found that we were far out

They came onto our ship, cutting down our sails and killing three of our men.

at sea. After a long time and a lot of hard work, we managed to get back to shore.

But the pirate captain decided to be more careful next time. He decided that he would not go out to sea without food and drink, and everything that he needed. He still had the little boat we had carried on our English ship. So he decided to use that boat for fishing. He told one of his slaves to build a cabin, or room, in the middle of the boat, where he could sleep and eat. And the pirate captain made sure that the boat was always full of food and drink and everything he might need.

One day the pirate captain told us that three important men from the town were coming fishing with us. He sent a lot of food and drink out onto the boat for the trip, and guns for shooting[30] birds. However, when everything was ready, the pirate captain told me that the men were not coming after all. They had decided they would eat at the captain's house instead. He wanted me to go with Xury and Moley to catch some fish for their dinner.

Suddenly I realized that I had a little ship – and at once I decided to try and escape. So I started getting ready, not for a fishing trip, but for a voyage. I brought more food and drink, candles and gunpowder[31], and put them on the boat. Then we left, sailing a little way out to sea.

We began fishing, but every time I caught a fish I secretly threw it back into the water.

'There are no fish here,' I said to Moley after a while. 'Let us go out to sea. We'll have more luck there.'

Moley agreed, and we went further away from the shore. Then I stopped the boat, as if I was ready to start fishing again. I pretended to reach forward for something behind Moley, then, surprising him, I pushed him over the side of the boat into the sea. He was a very good swimmer and I knew he would not drown[32]. He called out to me at first, asking me to take him back into the boat. Then he swam as fast as he could towards us. I took one of the guns and pointed it at his head.

'If you do what I say, I will not hurt you,' I told him. 'You swim well enough to reach the shore. Swim back to Sallee. If you come near the boat, I will shoot you through the head.'

He turned around and swam towards the shore. When he had gone, I turned towards the slave boy, Xury.

'Xury,' I said. 'You must promise to do everything I say. If you do not, I will throw you into the sea too.'

The boy promised to follow me as his master[33], and to come with me all over the world. So we sailed away down the coast of Africa, not stopping for five days. I wanted to get as far away as possible from the pirate captain and his people.

After this, we carried on down the coast, stopping only when we needed to find water. I knew that European ships came into the coast of Africa further south. I was hoping that we would meet one of these ships and that they would take us in. For miles and miles we saw nothing on the coast, and heard nothing apart from the terrible noises of wild animals at night.

Then one day, when I was in the cabin, I suddenly heard Xury cry out.

'Master!' he shouted. 'I see a ship!'

It was a Portuguese ship, and I was worried that it was going too fast for anyone to see us. But it suddenly slowed down. I fired my gun to show them that we needed help. And, seeing smoke, the ship stopped and waited for us. When we finally reached them, I told them that I had escaped from a pirate captain at Sallee. Hearing my story, they kindly took Xury and me into their ship, with all our things. I was so happy to be free, and I told the captain I would give him everything I had. But he kindly said that he would take nothing from me. And he promised to carry me to Brazil without asking me to pay.

When we got to Brazil, the captain very kindly bought our boat from me and also paid me some money for my slave boy

Xury. I did not want to sell poor Xury's freedom, when he had helped me to find my freedom. But the captain promised to free Xury in ten years time, if he became a Christian[34]. And, as Xury was happy to go, I let the captain take him.

3

I Am Shipwrecked

When we arrived in Brazil, I went to stay on a sugar plantation, where sugar plants are grown and sugar is made. The planters who owned the plantations were very rich, and I decided I would like to become a planter too.

I bought a small area of land, and grew a little more sugar each year, so that by the third year I needed help. But this was not the life I wanted. This was not why I had run away from my father's home. I often said to myself that I could have done this in England among friends and family. I wondered why I had come five thousand miles to work so hard in Brazil.

When the captain of the Portuguese ship went back to Europe, he kindly promised to send for some of my money from the widow in London. He then used the money to buy things which I could sell at a better price in Brazil. Suddenly I found that I had a lot of money. I used some of the money to get slaves to help me, and my plantation grew and grew.

I had a good life, but just as before, I could not be happy with it. I could have become rich in my new plantation, but I wanted to get richer quicker. So when a group of merchants and planters asked me to come to Africa with them, I agreed. I had told them about my voyages to Africa, and how easy it was to buy slaves there. And so they wanted to make a voyage to bring back enough slaves for their plantations.

Before I left Brazil I wrote a will to explain who my money should be given to if I died. I left everything I owned to the Portuguese captain who had saved my life. I also arranged for people to look after my plantation while I was away.

I left Brazil to go to Africa on the 1st of September 1659. We had a good trip at first, and although the weather was very hot, the sea was calm. But after two weeks, we were hit by a hurricane – a terrible storm with strong winds. For twelve days we were blown across the rough sea, expecting to die every day.

When the storm finally died down, we decided to sail towards Barbados. We knew that we couldn't go on to Africa because the ship had been badly hit by the winds and the sea. But as we sailed on, another storm hit us, and blew us far away. We were blown miles away from all the other merchant ships. We were not just in danger of dying at sea now. We had been blown into an area where cannibals – men who eat other people – lived. If we didn't drown at sea, we were in danger of being killed and eaten by cannibals!

When the wind was still blowing hard, early one morning, one of our men suddenly cried out 'Land!'. We all ran outside to look, and at that moment the ship hit sand[35]. She was stuck, and the waves broke over her so hard that we thought we would all die at any minute. We knew that the ship would break into pieces very soon. It is difficult to describe in words how terrified we all were.

There was a small boat on the ship, and at last we managed to get it into the sea. There were eleven of us, and we all climbed into the boat. But the sea was so high that we knew we would all drown. We could see land, but we did not know whether the land was an island. We did not know whether there were people on it, either. We rowed towards the land. But we knew that our boat would be broken into pieces by the huge waves breaking on the shore.

After we had rowed towards the shore for about four miles, a huge wave hit our boat. It knocked the boat over at once, and we were all thrown into the sea. I was carried towards the shore by the huge wave. I couldn't take a breath[36], and I was terrified.

As the wave died down, it went back, leaving me near the shore. I was half dead, but I got up and ran towards the land. But then another huge wave hit me, and I went right under again. I held my breath, and tried to swim towards the shore.

Just as I had no breath left, I felt myself going up, and my head came out above the water. Once again, the waves went back and I got to my feet and ran towards the shore. Two more times I was carried forward by huge waves. The last one threw me hard against a rock, and I held onto it until the wave had died down. Then I ran towards the shore once more. This time the waves that came over me were not so high, and did not knock me over[37]. So I was able to climb up the rocks onto the grass, safe from the sea.

17

I was alive! I could not believe that I was safe, and I thanked God for saving me. Then I looked all around me. Suddenly I saw that I was not as lucky as I had thought. I was wet, and I had no clothes or food and drink. I had no gun, and the other men from the ship had all drowned. For a while I ran around like a madman. Night was coming, and I was afraid I would be killed by wild animals. I walked up from the shore a little way to find some water to drink. And then I climbed into a tree so that I would be safe from wild animals, and fell asleep.

4

I Find Many Things for Myself

When I woke, it was morning. The storm had died down, and the sea was calm and blue. I was surprised to see that our ship had been carried by the waves off the sand and up towards the shore. This made me feel terribly sad once more. For I saw that we had done the wrong thing by leaving the ship. If we had stayed on it, the other men would all be alive now. And I would not be all alone.

I cried at this thought at first, but then I decided to go to the ship. I needed food and drink and clothes. I swam out to the ship, and climbed onto it. There I found that all the food and drink was still dry. I ate some biscuits and drank some rum, and then I made a small raft[38] from some large pieces of wood, to carry things off the ship. When the raft was ready, I looked around the ship for the things I would need. I took some more large pieces of wood, plenty of food and drink, clothes, tools[39], guns and two barrels[40] of gunpowder.

The sea was calm, and I managed to row back to the shore on my raft. There I found a little opening in the land, where there was a small river. I followed the river until I found a place where I could land the raft safely. And after nearly losing everything in the water several times, I at last brought the things from the ship safely onto land.

My next job was to find a safe place to stay and to keep all my things. I still did not know if anyone lived in this place. I did not even know whether it was an island or part of the mainland[41]. So I took a gun, and climbed to the top of a small hill just above the river. From the top I could see that I was on an island. I could see some rocks and two more small islands far away, but no other land. I could also see that nobody seemed to be living on the island. I guessed that there were probably wild animals, but I could not see any, although there were lots of birds.

When I got down from the hill, I made myself a small hut[42] from the barrels and pieces of wood I had brought from the ship. Then I started to think of the other things I could take from the ship which would be useful for me. I knew that as soon as there was another storm, the ship would break into pieces. So I decided to get everything I could from the ship before doing anything else. I swam back to the ship and made a second raft. I brought away some more tools and clothes, sheets, blankets, a telescope and some sails.

I brought the second raft safely onto the shore, and then made myself a little tent[43] using some of the sail and some pieces of wood. I brought all the clothes and food inside, put the empty barrels around the tent, and made myself a bed. And that night, tired from all my hard work, I slept very well.

Every day after that, I swam back out to the ship and brought back anything I could find. I took many things, including pens, paper, maps, three Bibles[44], and even the ship's dog and cats. After I had taken everything from inside the ship, I began to take pieces of iron[45] and metal rope from the ship itself. I took anything I felt might be useful. I had already made eleven little voyages to the ship and back again, and was returning for another one day when a wind started to blow. I went onto the ship anyway, and found some useful things and also some money. I smiled to myself when I saw the money. 'You are worth nothing to me!' I laughed. 'What can I use you for here?' But I took it with me anyway.

The wind blew hard all that night, and by the morning the ship had disappeared under the water. I was pleased that I had worked so hard to take everything out of the ship while I still could.

My next job was to find a safe place to live and keep my

things. I thought about this very carefully. I wanted to find a place that had fresh water and shade[46] from the hot sun. I also needed the place to be safe, as I still did not know if there were cannibals or wild animals on the island. I wanted to be near the sea, too. Then, if I saw a ship, I could light a fire and call for help.

At last I found a good place for my home. It was a flat piece of land on a steep[47] hill, and because the hill was so steep, I knew that nothing could come down at me from above. It was a safe place, with plenty of shade. At the back of the flat piece of land, against the hillside, there was a rocky wall with a hole in it like the entrance to a cave[48].

I cut some wood and made two strong fences[49] in a half-circle in front of the rocky wall. There were no doors in the fences. Instead, I came in and out using a ladder[50]. After I had climbed inside, I pulled the ladder over the top of the fence. This meant that no person or animal could easily get inside, and so I was able to sleep at night feeling safe.

Behind these fences, I made a large tent. I then brought all the things I had taken from the ship into my new hut. When I had done this, I dug out[51] the hole in the rocky wall at the back of my hut. I made it into a proper cave where I could keep things.

It took me many days, and a lot of hard work, to make the hut and get it how I wanted it. While I was making it, I also went out every day with my gun. I was pleased to find that there were goats[52] on the island. When they saw me they ran away quickly and I found it difficult to get near them at first. But then I noticed that they could not see me if I was up above them. So I quickly learned to climb up on the rocks and shoot from there, and after that I found it easy to kill them.

It was difficult for me to go on at times. I knew that I was hundreds of miles from the places merchant ships went to. I was sure that I was going to die on this lonely island, completely alone. When I thought about this, tears ran down my face. I felt sorry that I had been born. But after a while something in me always sent those feelings away. 'Weren't there eleven men in that ship?' a voice inside me would say. 'And didn't the others all die, while you were saved? Isn't it better to be here than under the sea?' Then I told myself how lucky I was in other ways too. I had been able to get lots of things from the ship, so that I had food, drink, clothes, guns and a tent.

After I had been on the island for about ten days, I realized that I would quickly forget what the date was. So I put up a large piece of wood on the shore where I had landed. I wrote the date I had arrived on the island on the wood: 30th September 1659. And then I made a mark on the wood with my knife for every day I stayed on the island, with a longer mark for the first day of every month.

*And then I made a mark on the wood with my knife for every day
I stayed on the island.*

5

I Become Very Ill

Over the next few months, I spent a lot of time making my hut bigger and better. I made a roof for the hut, and made the cave at the back of the hut much bigger, with a door. I began making shelves to put all my things on, and a table and chair. It was very difficult to make these things, as I had so few tools. But I had a lot of time.

I began to write a diary, and I started to break the day up into parts. In the morning, if it wasn't raining, I went out with my gun for two or three hours. Then I worked on my hut or my table or chair until lunchtime. After I had eaten, I slept for a couple of hours while it was very hot. Then in the evening I worked again. I had no candles, so at first I went to bed at about seven o'clock, when it got dark. But after a while, I learned to make candles out of goat fat. And then I was able to read or write my diary in the evenings.

A few months after I had arrived on the island, I was amazed[53] to find some corn[54] growing near my hut, and, later, some rice[55]. I could not believe it. I knew that corn did not normally grow in this part of the world. So for a while I felt sure that this was a present from God for me. Then I remembered that I had emptied corn from a bag from the ship. I had emptied it in the place where the corn was growing. I carefully saved the corn and rice that had grown. I wanted to plant it again so that I might be able to make bread one day.

One day, just after I had finished working on my hut, the top of my cave suddenly started falling in. I ran outside and saw at once that there was an earthquake[56]. The ground shook[57] three times, very hard, and the top of a huge rock near the sea fell down with the most terrible noise. I had never seen an

24

earthquake before, and I was terrified. I was sure that the hill would fall down on my tent, and all my things would be lost.

I was too scared to go back inside my tent, so I sat outside. After a while, a wind started to blow, getting stronger and stronger, and before long there was a hurricane. Trees were pulled up from the ground and the sea crashed on the shore. Then, after three hours, the storm started to die down and it began to rain very hard. I saw that this meant that the earthquake was over, so I went back into my cave. But I found it very difficult to sleep that night, or for the next few nights, and I lay awake worrying that the hill might fall on top of me.

A few days later, I found some pieces from the ship lying on the shore. I also found that the wreck of the ship had been broken open and pushed in towards the shore by the earthquake. This meant that when the sea was out, I could walk right up to the wreck. For the next few weeks, I went out to the wreck every day and took wood and iron and many useful things from it. One day, walking down to the wreck, I found a turtle[58]. It was the first turtle I had seen on the island, and I spent the next day cooking it. It was the best thing I had eaten since arriving there.

A couple of months after the earthquake, I became very ill with a fever[59]. I was sick for many days. I thought I would die, and prayed to God. Then on the ninth day of being ill, I had a dream that frightened me. In my dream I saw a man come down out of a black cloud, burning with fire. The man walked towards me with a knife in his hand, and I thought he was going to kill me. Then he spoke to me in a terrible voice.

'Many bad things have happened to you,' he said. 'But you have still not asked God to forgive you. Now, you will die.'

When I woke up, I thought about this dream. I remembered my father's words to me. 'If you go to sea, God will not be pleased with you,' he had warned me. He had told me I would be very sorry if I didn't listen to him. My father had been right.

25

I had not thought before that all the terrible things that had happened to me were perhaps because I had lived such a bad life as a young man. And I had not really thanked God for all the good things he had given to me. I decided then that I would pray to God, read the Bible and try to become a better person.

The next day, I made myself a medicine of tobacco and rum. I slept so deeply that night that I did not wake up until the next afternoon. I felt a little better that day, and when the fever came back, it was much lighter than before. I took my medicine every day, and after a few days the fever finally went. While I was getting better, I started to read the Bible every morning and night. I felt terribly sorry for the way I had lived my life. Now when I prayed to God I did not ask him to set me free from the island. I asked him to forgive me for the terrible things I had done.

6

I Travel Across the Island

Once I was well again, I decided to explore[60] the island. I had now been there for ten months, and I no longer felt that I had any chance of being set free. My hut was finished, and I wanted to see what I could find. I started by following the river where I had taken my rafts. Up the river there were lovely grass fields, with tobacco growing on the higher land. Further on, the river became much smaller and finally stopped, and I came into an area of woodland. There I was surprised to find grapes and melons growing. And continuing on, I came to a beautiful green area of the island which was full of orange, lemon and lime[61] trees. It was like a planted garden.

After three days away from my hut exploring this area and sleeping in trees, I returned home. I carried some grapes and limes with me. But I went back several times over the next month, collecting fruit. It was a beautiful area, and I began to wish that I had built my hut there. I thought about moving to that part of the island, but at last I decided that I should stay where I was. My hut was close to the sea, so if a ship ever came near the island, I would see it. There probably never was going to be a ship, but living where I was, I could still hope.

At last I decided to build another home in this beautiful place, so that I could have a country house and a seaside house. I spent several weeks making a little bower[62], with a strong fence around it, and I hung up lots of grapes to dry in the trees. They made excellent raisins, which I could keep for the winter.

I had just finished building my bower, and collecting all the raisins, when heavy rains came. I returned to my cave. Over the next two months there were many days when I could not go out at all because of the heavy rain.

On the 30th of September, I put another mark on the piece of wood on the shore where I had landed. I had now been on the island for a year. I spent the day praying to God and fasting – not eating or drinking anything.

———

After the rains, I decided to plant the rice and corn that I had picked and saved. But because it was so dry for the next few months, the plants did not come up until the next rains. So from then on, I learned to plant them just before the rains. I was starting to know now which months were rainy and which months were dry, so I got ready for the rains by finding lots of food. Then I could stay inside as much as possible when it was raining.

As I said before, I very much wanted to see the whole island. So towards the end of my second year there, I decided to go on

I spent several weeks making a little bower, and I hung up lots of grapes to dry in the trees.

from my bower to the seashore on the other side of the island. I took my gun, my dog, and plenty of gunpowder and food, and set off on my journey. A little way on from my bower, I came to a point where I could see the sea to the west. There, about fifty miles away, I could see land, which I guessed must be part of America. I thought it might be Spanish land. If it were, I might one day see a ship go past. But it could also be the land between the Spanish areas and Brazil, where cannibals lived. So once again I thanked God that I had not landed there.

I was still thinking about this as I walked on further. This side of the island was much nicer than my side, with fields full of flowers and lovely woods. There were also lots of parrots[63]. After trying several times, I managed to catch a young parrot. I wanted to take it home and teach it to speak to me.

I did not go far each day, but explored each little area very carefully. And at night I either slept in a tree or put up a little fence around myself on the ground. On the shore I found many turtles, and different kinds of bird. I continued along the coast for several miles, and then put up a large wooden stick in the sand. I had decided that for my next journey I would go along the shore from my hut until I came to the stick.

When I got back to my hut, I was very pleased to arrive 'home', as I had been away for more than a month. I spent a week resting there, and made a home for my little parrot, which I called Poll.

When the 30th of September came once more, and I had been on the island for two years, I spent the day thanking God. I used to sit crying like a baby sometimes when I thought about my life. I did not know if I would ever leave the island or see people again. But now I could see that this was a much happier life than my old bad one. I read the Bible every day. And I always found words there which made me feel better.

7

I Make Myself a Canoe[64]

By the end of December in my third year on the island, I was able to pick my rice and corn. They had grown well, and I was very pleased that I might one day have bread. But first I had to find a way to make the bread. I decided to re-plant all the corn so that I would have an even bigger crop[65]. I spent a week making a wooden spade[66] so that I could get the land ready. Then I planted the corn in two large areas near my hut, and put in hedges[67] around them.

There were many things I needed to make my own bread. So while the corn was growing, I spent the next few months making them. The first things I needed were some pots. So when it was raining, and I could not go out, I spent hours trying to make them. I must have made hundreds of pots that I had to throw away. Some of them would not stand up. Some of them cracked under the sun. And some of them just fell into pieces when I picked them up. But at last, after about two months, I made two good large pots. And after that, I learned how to heat the pots in my fire so that they would hold water.

No one would believe how happy I was to have a pot that I could cook in. Before the first pots were even cold, I put one of them on the fire again and made myself a soup. It was a very good soup, even though I did not have all the things I needed.

My next job was to find a way of grinding[68] the corn. I found a large piece of wood, and spent a long time cutting it into the right shape. Then I burned and cut a hole in the middle. And finally I cut another large piece of wood so that I could grind the corn.

Whenever I was working inside like this, I spent a lot of time talking to my parrot Poll. He quickly learned to say his own name, and so 'Poll' was the first word I heard spoken on the island by anyone other than myself.

I spent most of my third year on the island making these things, and looking after my corn. The rest of my time was spent reading the Bible, hunting[69] for food and cooking. I made a kind of bread oven[70], and when the corn grew, I baked my own bread for the first time.

———

All this time, I did not stop thinking about the land that I had seen from the other side of the island. I did not think about the dangers of being caught by a cannibal and killed. I only thought of trying to escape from the island. I therefore decided to make myself a canoe. First I cut down a large tree. It took me nearly a month to cut it down, and to take off the branches. It took me another month to cut it into the right shape. And it took me three months to cut out the inside. I worked very hard on it, and when at last it was ready, I was very pleased with it. It was a very good canoe. But like a fool, I had never thought about how I would get it into the sea. I tried everything, but I could not get the canoe into the water because it was too heavy. I was very upset about this. Now I saw, too late, that it was foolish to begin a job without thinking about it properly.

In the middle of this work, I finished my fourth year on the island. Once again, I felt very thankful. I could call myself king of the whole island. I had all the food I needed – goats, turtles, wild birds, grapes and now bread too. I had now learned to think about all the good things in my life instead of the bad things. I had learned to think about all the things I had, and not all the things I wanted or needed.

For the next five years, I lived in very much the same way, growing rice and corn and drying my raisins. But I also spent a long time making another canoe. I made this canoe much smaller than the first, so that I could get it into the water. It was much too small to take me across to the land I had seen from the other side of the island. But I very much wanted to make a voyage around the island and see the rest of the coast.

I spent a long time getting my canoe ready for my voyage. I made a sail for it, and some boxes to keep food and drink dry. And at last, on the 6ᵗʰ of November, in my sixth year on the island, I set out. I took some bread, half a goat, some rice and some rum, my gun and two coats to lie on. The island was not big, but when I came to the east side, I found that there were rocks going far out into the sea at that point. There were some very strong currents[71] around the rocks, and the wind was blowing hard, so I waited there for two days. On the third day, when the sea was calm, I sailed away again. But the currents were so strong that my little boat was pulled far out to sea.

Suddenly my lonely island seemed to me like the loveliest place in the world. I had thought my life on the island was unhappy, but I was wrong. It would be much worse to be lost at sea in a little boat. I knew that I would soon die when I had no food or drink left. But I couldn't see how I could ever get back to the island again. There was no wind for sailing. And although I tried to row back to the island, the currents were too strong.

Then, around lunchtime, I suddenly felt a little wind blowing up. It grew stronger and stronger, and I started to sail back towards the island. I was a long way from it by now. On a cloudy day, I would not have been able to find my way back. But luckily the sky was clear. I sailed away from the currents, and by the afternoon, I started to come near to the north side of the island – the opposite side from my hut. The wind continued to blow, and I could not believe how lucky I was. At last I came onto the shore. And when I got out of the boat I fell down on my knees and thanked God.

The next morning, I found a place to keep my canoe further up the coast. I realised that I was not far from the place I had walked to on this side of the island before. So I set off towards my bower, arriving there by the evening. I lay down and fell asleep at once. When I woke up, someone was calling 'Robin Crusoe! Where are you, Robin Crusoe? Where have you been?' I thought I was dreaming at first, but when I woke up properly, I could still hear the voice. I was terribly frightened for a moment, but then I opened my eyes and saw Poll on top of the hedge. He flew over to me and sat on my hand, calling 'Poor Robin Crusoe! How did you come here? Where have you been?'. He seemed very pleased to see me, and we set off home together.

8

I Find a Footprint in the Sand

For a while after that, I lived very quietly. I became very good at making things out of wood, and at making pots. And after a long time, I had also learned how to make very good baskets[72]. But when I had been on the island for eleven years, I became worried that I had only a little gunpowder left. So my most important job now was to catch some goats and tame[73] them. I hoped that I could keep tame goats and then kill them without using my gun.

I made some large holes in the ground and then covered them over. I hoped that a goat would fall into one of the holes when it walked over the cover. I didn't catch anything at first, so I changed the holes and covers. And one morning I found three baby goats in the holes. I tied them up and took them to my bower, and then made a large enclosure, or area of fenced-in land, for them. I fed them every day, and they quickly became tame. After a year and a half, I had twelve tame goats, so now, as well as goat's meat, I also had milk, butter and cheese.

When I killed a goat, I dried its skin, and I used the skins to make clothes for myself. I often looked at myself and smiled. 'What would everyone think if I dressed like this in England?' I thought. I had a big goatskin hat and a goatskin coat and trousers. I carried a basket on my back, and a gun on my shoulder. I had a long moustache[74], and over my head I held a big ugly goatskin umbrella that I had made.

At the back of my hut, I had dug out lots of caves in the rock, where I kept my corn and rice in large pots. The hedges around my hut had now grown so tall that no one would ever guess there was a hut behind them. And near my hut were the two pieces of land where I grew my corn.

At my country home, my tent was also hidden behind a large hedge. I kept my goats here and dried my grapes. And I often visited my canoe to make sure it was safe. Sometimes I took it out in the water, but I never went far from the shore. I was too frightened of being carried away from the island again by winds or currents.

One day, when I was going to the place where I kept my boat, I suddenly saw a footprint[75] in the sand. I stopped dead and looked around me. I couldn't hear anything or see anything. I went up and down the shore, but there were no other footprints. Then I came back to the same place. Perhaps it wasn't a footprint at all. Perhaps I had made a mistake. But no, I could clearly see the shape of a foot.

I hurried home, feeling terrified. I kept looking behind me to see if someone was following me. I imagined that someone

was hiding behind every bush. When I got home, I ran into my hut like a frightened rabbit.

I did not sleep that night. I lay awake in my bed thinking about the footprint. I decided that cannibals must have come to the island from the mainland. Had they found my boat, I wondered? Would they come back looking for me? And if they didn't find me, would they take away my tame goats and dig up my corn fields? For three days, I did not go out of my hut. I was too frightened even to milk my goats. But after reading the Bible and praying, I at last started to feel braver. Perhaps it was actually my own footprint, I told myself. After a few days, I felt brave enough to go back to the shore and look at the footprint again. But I realized at once that it could not possibly be my footprint. It was much bigger than my foot. Again I hurried home, terrified.

But after a good sleep, I started to think sensibly. I had lived here for fifteen years, and never seen anybody. So if anyone did come to the island, they must go away again very quickly. And therefore I just needed to make myself safe in case I saw any more cannibals.

36

First, I built another wall around my hut, and planted lots of trees in front of it – so after five or six years, there was a thick wood in front of my hut. No one could have guessed that anyone was living behind the wood. And because the only way into my hut was over two ladders, no one could get in without hurting themselves.

I also made a second enclosure and moved a few goats there. I wanted to be sure that if anything happened to my goats, I had others to keep me alive. I started looking for a third enclosure too.

Two years after I had seen the footprint in the sand, I was out looking for a third enclosure when I saw a boat on the sea, many miles away. I was in a part of the island where I had never been before. And when I came down to the shore there, I saw the most terrible sight. I saw the hands, feet and bones[76] of dead people lying on the sand. I could see where there had been a fire. Cannibals had come to the island to cook and eat people. I could not believe what I was seeing, and I was suddenly sick. I could not stay there, so I walked back home, praying. I thanked God that I had not been born in a part of the world where cannibals lived. And I thanked him for everything I had on the island.

For the next two years, I did not go far from my hut, my bower or my second goat enclosure. I stopped using my gun, because I was afraid that if cannibals had come to the island they would hear it. But after a while I became very angry with the cannibals. I hated the idea of people eating each other. I decided that the next time the cannibals came to my island I would fight them. I would save the person they were going to eat.

I thought about this for hours, and sometimes I dreamed about it. I found a place on the hillside where I could watch for their boats without being seen. I got my guns ready, and every day, for two or three months, I looked out for them.

But I saw nothing, and after a while, my thoughts began to change. The cannibals did not understand that it was wrong to eat people. And they had done nothing against me. It was not my job to punish[77] them for what they were doing. I realized that I was putting myself in a lot of danger too. If I did not kill all the cannibals, one of them might escape. And he might then come back with others to kill me for what I had done. I thanked God that he had made me see that my idea of killing the cannibals was wrong.

9

I Hear the Sound of a Man's Voice

I was very careful now not to make a lot of noise on the island. I also tried not to make a lot of smoke[78], so that if there were cannibals on the island, they would not see it.

One day, when I was cutting wood near my second goat enclosure, I found a large hole in the ground, hidden behind a big branch. The hole led[79] into an underground cave. It was dark and dry, and when I lit a candle, thousands of lights shone back from the walls. There was something in the rock – gold, perhaps. I was very pleased to find the cave, as it made a very good hiding place for some of my guns and gunpowder. I also told myself that if the cannibals ever saw me, I could run away and hide in the cave. They would never find me there.

I had been on the island for twenty-three years by now. I was used to living there. And I was happy to spend the rest of my life there. My parrot Poll now spoke very well, and I liked having him with me. My dog was a loving friend for sixteen years until he died. And I also kept two or three tame cats and some seabirds as well.

I was very happy with my life – I only wished that I could be safe from the cannibals.

One night in May, in my twenty-fourth year on the island, there was a very bad storm. I was in my hut when I suddenly heard the sound of a gun. I jumped up and ran up the hill at the back of my hut, where I heard the gun once more. The sound came from the sea. It was a ship calling for help.

I got some dry wood and lit a big fire. I wanted the people on the ship to know I was here. I hoped they might be able to help me. I kept the fire going all night. When day came, I could see something a long way away, in the sea, through my telescope. It wasn't moving, but I wasn't sure whether it was a ship. Taking my gun, I ran across the island towards the rocks where I had been carried away by the current in my canoe. From there, I could clearly see the wreck of a ship on the rocks. I felt terribly sad for the men on the ship. And I felt terribly sad for myself too. After so many years, other people had come so near to the island. Suddenly I wanted more than anything else to be with other people again. 'If only one of them had lived!' I cried to myself, again and again.

A few days later, when the sea was calm again, I decided to go out to the wreck in my canoe. I got my little boat ready and I started out to sea. The first day I could not reach the ship and I came back quickly. I was terrified of being carried out to sea by the currents again. But on the second day, after watching the currents carefully, I managed to reach the ship.

It was a Spanish ship, and it had been broken apart by the rocks. When I came close to it, a dog appeared. It cried out when it saw me, and swam to my boat, where I gave it bread and water.

When I climbed into the wreck, I found two dead men holding on to each other, but no other people. I took some food and drink, gunpowder, clothes and money from the wreck, and then rowed back to the island. But seeing a ship come so close

had made me want to escape once more. And for the next two years, I could not stop thinking of how I could get away. If the cannibals could come to my island, I thought, then I could surely reach the mainland where they lived. I didn't think about what would happen to me if they caught me.

One night I dreamed that the cannibals came back to my island. In my dream, I saved the man that they were going to kill and eat. He was very thankful, and became my servant[80]. I saw that he could help me to escape from the island. He could tell me where to go and what to do. I woke up feeling very happy, until I remembered that this was all a dream.

However, the dream had given me an idea. I needed someone to help me escape from the island. I decided to try and save a man from the cannibals so that he could help me. I knew that I would have to kill a lot of men to do this. And for a long time I worried about this a lot. I did not want to kill people. I knew that it was wrong. But I had to escape.

I went out to the other side of the island to look for the cannibals almost every day. Now that I knew what I was going to do, I wanted them to come. But for more than a year and a half, I saw nothing.

Then, one morning, I saw five canoes on the shore on my side of the island. I went to the top of my hill with my telescope. From there I could see that there were more than thirty cannibals. They had built a fire and they were dancing around it. As I watched, I saw the cannibals take two prisoners[81] out of a boat. They knocked one man down, and then they started to cut him up while the other man waited.

Suddenly the other man saw that he had a chance, and started to run across the sand. He was running towards my part of the island. I felt terribly frightened when I saw where he was running. I was afraid that the cannibals would all follow him and find my hut. But then I saw that there were only three cannibals coming after him.

When he came to the river, the prisoner swam quickly across. Two of the cannibals followed him, more slowly, but the third cannibal could not swim. He turned and went back to the shore. Suddenly I saw that I had a chance to get a servant for myself, as I had dreamed. I ran back to my hut to get my guns, and then ran down the hill towards the men.

'Stop!' I shouted to the prisoner. Then I ran towards the first cannibal and knocked him down with my gun. He fell to the ground. The other cannibal saw me and took out his bow and arrow[82] to shoot at me. But I fired my gun and killed him at once.

The prisoner was so frightened by my gun that he did not move. He looked as if he was going to run away again. I called to him, and he came a little way and then stopped. He came very slowly, and he kept kneeling down[83] in the sand to thank me for saving his life. I could see that he was shaking with fear. I smiled at him and tried to look very friendly. At last he came

The other cannibal saw me and took out his bow and arrow to shoot at me.

close to me. He kissed the ground by my feet, and then picked up my foot and put it on his head. He was trying to show me that I was his master and he was my slave.

I helped him to stand up and showed him that I was very happy with him. But then I saw that the cannibal I had knocked down was moving. I pointed at him and showed my new servant. He said something, and although I could not understand his words, I liked hearing them. It was the first time I had heard another man's voice for more than twenty-five years. My new servant pointed at my sword[84]. I gave it to him and he cut off the cannibal's head quickly and easily. Then he brought the head and put it next to my feet with the sword, making lots of signs[85] which I did not understand.

Then my new servant went to look at the first man I had killed. He turned the body over and looked at the place where I had shot him. He could not believe it. He made signs to show that he wanted to bury the men in the sand. If any of the other cannibals followed, we did not want them to see the bodies. He dug two big holes in the sand and quickly buried the two dead men. When they were buried, I took him to the cave in the woods where I kept my guns. I gave him some water, bread and raisins and showed him where to lie down. He quickly fell asleep.

10

I Call Him Friday

My new servant was a tall, good-looking man, and about twenty-six years old, I thought. He had a very good face, manly but soft, and long black hair. His skin was very dark, and he had a small nose, bright eyes and thin lips. He looked like a good person.

After he had slept for half an hour, he came out of the cave and ran towards me. He made lots of signs to show me how thankful he was. He put his head on the ground again and put my foot on top of it. He wanted to show me that he would work for me for the rest of his life.

I told him that I would call him Friday, because that was the day when I saved his life. I taught him to call me 'Master', and to say 'yes' and 'no', and then I gave him some bread and milk.

We stayed in the cave all night, and in the morning I took Friday back to my hut. When we came to the place where the two cannibals were buried in the sand, Friday stopped. He made signs that we should dig the men up and eat them. But I showed him that that made me very angry. I showed him that it made me feel sick. And I told him to come away. He understood, and followed me to the top of the hill. I wanted to see if the cannibals had gone.

I could see where the men had been, but they had gone and so had their canoes. However, I wanted to be sure. So, taking Friday with me, I went down to the shore. When we got there, my blood turned cold. It was a horrible sight for me, although Friday was not worried by it at all. The shore was covered with half-eaten flesh[86] and bones, and the ground was red with blood. I made Friday pick everything up and burn it. And I made signs to show him again that I would kill him if he ate people. I saw that he understood me.

When we got back to my hut, I found some clothes for Friday, and made him a goatskin jacket and hat. Then I made a little tent for him, between the two fences around my hut. I wanted to feel safe at night. To get into my hut, Friday would have to climb over the fence or break down the door. And that would make so much noise that it would wake me up.

I should not have worried, though. No man could ever have had such a loving and honest servant as Friday. And he showed me many times that he would happily give his life to save mine. I began to teach him many things. Most importantly, I taught him to understand me and to speak to me. He learned so quickly, and enjoyed learning so much, that I loved talking to him. My life seemed so good. If only I felt safe from the cannibals, I thought to myself, I would be happy to stay on the island forever.

I decided to kill a goat so that Friday could eat animal flesh. But he was terrified of my gun, and when I shot the goat, he could not believe it. He shook all over, and I thought he was going to fall to the ground. Then he came and kneeled down in front of me, talking. I could see that he was asking me not to kill him. I laughed, and tried to show him that I would not hurt him. Then I showed him that I was going to shoot a parrot. When he saw the parrot fall, he was terrified again. He would not touch my gun for several days, but I often found him talking to it. He told me later that he was asking it not to kill him.

When I cooked the goat, Friday liked the meat very much. He told me that he would never eat a man's flesh again. And I was very glad to hear this.

I taught Friday how to make bread, and very soon he could do it as well as me. Because there were two of us on the island now, I decided that we needed to grow more corn. So I found a new area of land, and showed Friday how to make a fence around it. He worked very hard and very happily.

———

This was the happiest year I had spent on the island. Friday began to speak English very well. I enjoyed talking to him, and I enjoyed being with him too. I really began to love my servant – and I believe he loved me more than anything in the world.

I learned from him that the land we could see from the island was Trinidad. I asked him all about his country and his people, and about the sea and the coast. I asked him how we could get to his country, and he told me we could go in a big canoe. When I heard this, I started to hope that Friday would one day help me to escape from the island.

I also talked about God with Friday, and I taught him about the Christian religion. Friday was very clever and asked me many questions about my religion. To answer his questions, I had to learn and think a lot myself. And I saw how lucky I was. My life on the island had helped me to know God. And now I was helping a poor cannibal to know God too.

11

We Fight Against the Cannibals

One day Friday told me about some white men who had arrived in his land in a boat. He told me that he and his people had saved the men from drowning.

'Where are they now?' I asked him. He told me that they still lived there, and that they had been there for about four years.

'Why didn't your people eat them?' I asked.

'They only eat people who come to fight with them,' Friday told me.

One day, a long time after this, we were on top of the hill on the east side of the island when we saw the mainland. Friday started to jump and dance around, happily.

'That is my land!' he cried. 'My country!'

His face was so full of happiness that it made me think. If Friday could one day get back to his own country, would he forget about his new Christian religion, I asked myself? Would he forget everything he had promised me? And would he come back with other men from his country and eat me? When I asked him these things, the poor man was very upset. He said that if he went back to his country, he would teach the people to pray to God. He would teach them never to eat men again. I told him that I would make him a canoe so that he could go home. But he said he would only go if I went with him.

'Me?' I said. 'But they will eat me if I go there.'

'No, no,' he said. 'I will stop them from eating you. I will make them love you.' He told me that they would love me because I had saved his life. And he told me how kind they were to the seventeen white men who had arrived in their boat.

After this, I decided that we should go across to the mainland, and, together with the white men, try to get back to Europe. I told Friday that we were going to make a new canoe. I told him that he would be able to go back home. But Friday did not say anything. He looked very sad.

'Why are you angry with me?' he said. 'What have I done?'

'I am not angry with you,' I told him.

'Then why are you sending me away to my country?'

'Friday, didn't you say that you wished you were there?'

'Yes, yes,' he said. 'But I wish we were both there.' He would not think of going home without me.

'No, Friday,' I said. 'What could I do there? You go home, and I will live here by myself again.'

Hearing this, Friday suddenly brought me a sword.

'Kill me,' he said. 'Don't send me away, kill me.' There were tears in his eyes. I saw then how much he loved me. And I promised him that I would never send him away from me.

So after this, we looked for a tree that would make a canoe big enough to carry us both to the mainland. I taught Friday how to use my tools and we worked together for about a month making the canoe. Then, while Friday made a mast[87], I made a sail.

Friday could row very well, but he had never seen a sail before. However, he learned quickly once more, and soon became a very good sailor. I had been on the island for twenty-seven years now, and Friday had been with me for three years. I felt sure that I would leave the island this year. But I went on planting my crops, looking after my goats and drying my grapes.

When the rainy season came, we found a safe place for the canoe and covered it with branches. I had decided that we should try to escape from the island in November or December. So now we just had to wait.

Once the rains stopped, we began getting ready for our voyage. I was busy one morning preparing food to take with

48

us, when Friday suddenly came running into the hut. 'Master! Master!' he cried. He looked very scared.

'What is the matter, Friday?' I said.

He told me that he had seen six canoes on the shore. He was terrified that the men had come back to look for him. He was afraid that they would cut him up and eat him.

I got my guns and swords ready, and then I climbed up the hill. From there I could see that there were twenty-one cannibals and three prisoners. They were very close to my side of the island, and I felt so angry that suddenly I wanted to kill them all.

'Friday!' I said, when I came back down to the hut. 'Will you come with me and kill these bad people?'

'Yes, master,' he replied. 'I will die when you tell me!'

Taking our guns, we set off towards the coast. But while we were walking, I began once more to feel that it was wrong for me to kill these cannibals. They had done nothing to hurt me. I decided that I would watch them. If God wanted me to do something, then I would listen to his call.

I had seen from the hill that the cannibals were on a part of the coast where the woods came down close to the sea. When we got to the woods we went forward slowly and quietly, until we were close to the men. I asked Friday to go slowly up to a big tree. From there he could see what they were doing.

He came back very quickly. He said the cannibals were already eating one prisoner and another lay tied up[88] on the ground. They would eat him next. He told me the man tied up on the ground was one of the white men who lived in his land.

I could not believe it. I went up to the big tree and looked. Friday was right. The man on the ground was a European. While I was watching, two cannibals got up and came towards him. I had to do something quickly.

'Friday,' I said. 'Are you ready? Fire the gun when I tell you.'

Friday took up his gun, and so did I.

'Fire!' I cried.

Friday killed two of the cannibals and hurt three more, and I killed one and hurt two. The other cannibals ran around, terrified. They did not understand about guns, and they did not know what was happening.

We fired again, and hurt many more of them. They ran around crying and shouting, covered in blood.

'Now, Friday, follow me,' I said.

We ran out of the wood, shouting loudly. Some of the cannibals ran and jumped into their canoes. I told Friday to shoot at them, while I ran to the poor man on the ground. I untied his hands and feet, and gave him some rum and a little bread.

He told me that he was Spanish, and I gave him a gun and a sword.

'We will talk later,' I said in Spanish. 'Now we must fight.'

The man was very weak[89], but he got up at once and started fighting. The cannibals were so terrified that they fell quickly, and soon they were nearly all dead. But four of them had managed to swim to the canoes, and were rowing away as fast as they could. I ran to one of the canoes, hoping to follow them and shoot at them. But when I jumped in, I found another man tied up by his hands and feet in the bottom of the boat. I untied him, but he could not stand or speak. I could see that he thought I was going to kill him. I gave him some rum, and told Friday to explain to him that he was safe. But when Friday saw the man's face, he began to jump about and cry. He kissed the man, and put his arms around him. Then he laughed and sang, and cried again. I watched, amazed. Friday could not speak for a while, or tell me what was happening. But at last, when he was a little calmer again, he told me that the man was his father.

Friday was so happy to see his father. He could not believe that he had nearly died, and had been saved. He held his

We ran out of the wood, shouting loudly.

father's head, and rubbed[90] his feet, full of love for him. It was too late now to follow the cannibals in the canoe, who had gone a long way already. I gave Friday some raisins for his father. He then ran all the way back to our hut to fetch some bread and water for him.

The Spanish man was resting under a tree. Because his feet had been tied up, and he had then fought against the cannibals, he could not even stand up. I told Friday to bring him some bread and water too, and to rub his feet like he had done for his father. Both men were too weak to walk. So Friday carried the Spanish man to the canoe where his father was lying. Then he brought the canoe round the coast and up the river, closer to our hut. We made something that the men could both lie on, and then carried them back to our home.

We could not carry them over the ladder inside the hut, so we decided to make a tent outside the fence from branches and old sails. Then we made beds for the men.

12

We Stop a Mutiny[91]

So now I had people on my island. I felt like a king. I had saved the lives of all my people, and I knew that they would die for me. I told Friday to kill a goat, and then made some soup, which we all ate together. Then Friday went back to the coast to get our guns.

The next day, I sent him back to the beach to bury the cannibals and clean up the flesh and bones. Then I had a little talk with my two new people. I asked Friday whether his father thought the cannibals would come back with more men. A big storm had blown up after the four cannibals had left in their canoe. Friday's father said he thought they had probably died at sea. But he said that if they did get back home, they would probably never come back. They did not understand about guns. They thought they had been attacked by thunder and lightning[92], not by men. Friday's father thought they would be too frightened ever to come back. And he was right. I heard later that the four men did get back home safely. And because of what had happened to them, none of their people ever came to the island again.

At the time, though, I did not know this. For a while, we were all afraid that the cannibals might come back. But day after day, no canoes came, and we started to feel less frightened. I began to think again about making a voyage across to the mainland. The Spanish man told me that there were sixteen of his men on the mainland. He said that although Friday's people treated them well, they had no gunpowder and little food. And they could not make a boat because they had no tools.

I asked him if he thought his men would like to come to my island. I told him that we could make a boat and escape together. But I also told him that I was afraid of being badly treated. I was worried that they might try to take me to Spain. And I would be killed because I was English and had a different religion.

The Spanish man promised that this would not happen. He was very grateful to me because I had saved him from the cannibals. He said the other men were all good men, and that they would be grateful to me too. Because they had no food or clothes or gunpowder, they needed help very badly. He was sure that if I helped them, they would be happy to die for me. And he said that if I wanted, he would go back to the mainland with Friday's father. He would talk to the men and make them promise to follow me.

First, though, we needed to grow more food. If the Spanish

men did come to the island, we would have to feed them, and we would need food for our voyage. So for several months, the four of us worked very hard. We dug more land and planted more crops. We went out every day to catch more goats so we would have meat and milk. And we collected lots of grapes and left them to dry in the hot sun. We also made many baskets for keeping food in.

At last we had enough food for everybody. I gave Friday's father and the Spanish man two guns and lots of food, and they set off to the mainland in a canoe. I had told the Spanish man that he could only bring people back to my island if they first made a promise. They had to promise not to hurt me, and to do everything I told them.

_____

The men had only been gone for eight days when something very strange happened. I was asleep one morning when Friday came running in, shouting.

'Master, master,' he cried. 'They have come back.'

I got up and ran outside through my little wood. I could see a boat with a sail coming towards the island. But it was not coming from the mainland.

'It is not the men we are waiting for,' I told Friday. 'We must be careful. We do not know if these people are friends or enemies.'

I went back to my hut and climbed up to the top of the hill with my telescope. I could see a ship a long way out at sea. It was an English ship, and the boat coming towards the island was an English boat. I did not know what to think. I was so happy to see an English ship. But something told me that I needed to be careful. What was an English ship doing here? My island was not near any of the places where English merchant ships went. And there had been no storms to blow the ship in here.

I was right to be careful. When the boat came in, I could

see that something was wrong. There were eleven men, but three of them were tied up. The three men were prisoners. I could not understand what was happening.

'Master, master,' Friday said. 'Look, the English men eat prisoners too.'

'No, Friday,' I said. 'They will not eat them, but I am afraid they will kill them.'

I watched the men. The three prisoners had sat down on the beach, but the others were running around looking at the island. The sea had gone out leaving their boat on the sand. I knew that they would not be able to leave the island for another ten hours.

I decided to get ready to fight. I put on my goatskin coat and my big cap, and I hung my sword at my side with two guns. I hung two guns over each shoulder as well, and gave several guns to Friday.

In the early afternoon, when it got very hot, the men went into the woods. I guessed that they were probably sleeping. The three prisoners were too frightened to sleep, however. They were sitting together under a big tree, so I decided to go and talk to them. I wanted to find out what was happening.

They were very surprised to see me come out of the woods. I looked very strange in my goatskin coat and big hat, with my sword and guns.

'Do not be surprised,' I said in English. 'You have a friend here. What has happened to you? How can we help you?'

The men were frightened by me at first. But after some time they told me their story. One of the men was the captain of the English ship I had seen. There had been a mutiny on the ship – the men had turned against the captain and taken over the ship themselves.

'They were going to kill me,' the captain said. 'But now they have decided to leave me on this island to die with these two men – my mate[93] and one of the passengers[94].'

'Where are the men now?' I asked.

The captain pointed to the trees where they were all sleeping.

'Do they have guns?' I asked.

'They have two guns, and another which they have left in the boat,' he replied.

I asked him if we should kill all the men, or take them prisoners. He said that two of the men were very bad, but the others would probably turn back to him. So I told the captain that I would help him if he promised two things.

'Firstly,' I said, 'You must do what I say on this island. You are not the captain here. Secondly, if we can get your ship back, you must take me to England.'

The captain was happy to agree to this. I gave him and his men some guns and we moved towards the men who were sleeping in the woods. As we got near, one of the men woke up and cried out to the others. But the captain and his two men were ready, and fired. They killed both the men who had led the mutiny.

The others now saw that there was nothing they could do. The captain told them he would not kill them if they promised to follow him once more. He made them agree that they had done terrible things. They all promised to be true to him, and he was happy to let them live. But I made him tie up their hands and feet while they were on the island.

13

We Recapture the Ship

When we were safe I told the captain my story. He was amazed to hear about my life on the island. I took him, his mate and the passenger to my hut, and gave them food and drink. They could not believe the things I told them and showed them. The captain particularly liked my hut, and the way it was completely hidden. The trees around it had been growing for twenty years now, and the wood was so thick that there was only one way through it to my hut.

I told the captain about my country bower, and promised to show it to him another time. But now we had to decide how to get the ship back. The captain told me that there were twenty-six men on the ship. They had all been part of the mutiny, so they would be afraid of being punished. They would therefore fight to the end. And there were not enough of us to fight against so many men.

I decided we must do something quickly. We thought that some more men from the ship would probably come looking for the others soon. We didn't want them to take their boat back. So we took everything out of it and made a hole in the bottom. Now it could not be used.

We had just finished, when we heard the ship fire a gun. The men on the ship were calling the other men back. We watched them through my telescope. When there was no answer, they put another boat into the water. There were ten men coming towards the island, and they all had guns.

'Who are these men?' I asked the captain.

He told me that three of them were good men, but that the others had all behaved very badly. He was terribly afraid that they would be too strong for us.

57

As soon as the boat set off, we asked Friday to take two of the prisoners to my cave. Two men were left tied up, but the other two, who the captain said were good men, promised to live or die with us. Now there were seven of us ready to fight, all of us with guns.

When the men landed, they ran over to the other boat. They were very surprised when they saw that it was empty with a hole in the bottom. They shouted for the other men, and fired their guns in the air, but nobody answered.

They went back to their boat, and at first we thought they were all going to go back to the ship. But after a while, seven of the men came back to the island, while three men stayed in the boat a little way out from the shore.

The seven men climbed up the little hill above my hut, and shouted again for the other men. They waited there for a long time, and then at last they started to walk back down towards the shore. It seemed that they had decided to go back to the ship without the others.

The captain, seeing this, was terrified that we would never get his ship back. But I had had an idea. I told Friday and the captain's mate to go down to the shore near the little river and shout to the men. I hoped that the men would follow the shouts, and that Friday and the mate would be able to lead the men deep into the woods.

The men were just getting into their boat when they heard Friday and the mate shouting. They ran along the shore towards the voices, but when they came to the river it was too high to cross. They called for the men in the boat to come and row them across the river. Then they tied the boat up there, left two men with it and ran on into the woods. This was just what I had wanted. We ran down and surprised the men at the boat, knocking one down with a gun. The other man had not been one of the main people in the mutiny, and he was happy to throw down his gun and join with us.

All this time, Friday and the captain's mate were making the men run all over the island. They kept shouting to them and then running deeper into the wood. When they finally came back to their boat, after several hours, they were very tired. When they saw that their boat was empty, they could not believe it. They were very frightened, and were sure that they were going to be killed or eaten up.

When it was nearly dark, the captain and Friday went as close as they could to the men. The man who had led the mutiny was very near to them, so they shot him and one other dead. Hearing the shooting, I moved forwards with our men, and told one of them to call out to the others.

'Put down your guns and talk to us, or you will die,' one of our men called, through the darkness.

Then the captain told the men that there was a governor[95] on the island, waiting to come and get them with fifty men. He told them that if they put down their guns they could live. The men did as they were told, and our men tied them up. We put three of the worst men in the cave, and tied up the others at my bower. The captain spoke to the men at the bower. He told them that when they got back to England they would all be killed for taking part in a mutiny. But he said that if they helped to get the ship back, the island's 'governor' would ask for them to be forgiven. Terrified, the men all fell down to their knees and promised to give their lives for the captain. They agreed to do whatever he told them.

We decided that the captain and his mate would take some of the men and try to recapture the ship. The others were kept behind as prisoners. We told the men who went with the captain that they must do as he said. If they didn't, the governor would kill the prisoners.

We fixed the hole in the first boat, and the captain and his mate left with their men in the two boats. Friday and I stayed behind with the prisoners. The captain had told me that if he took back the ship he would fire seven guns. And at two o'clock in the morning, I heard the guns firing from the ship. I had been waiting on the shore all night, and when I heard the guns I finally went to sleep.

In the morning, I was woken by the captain. When I climbed to the top of the hill, he pointed to the ship out at sea and put his arm around me.

'My dear friend,' he said. 'There's your ship – she is yours. And so are we, and everything that is inside her.' I could not speak, and I thought I might fall to the ground. I knew the time had finally come for me to leave the island. I felt so happy that I started to cry.

The captain gave me a drink and helped me to sit down. I put my arms around him. I told him that God had sent him to

save me. And I thanked God, who had given me so much on the island and was now setting me free at last.

The captain brought me many presents from the ship – bottles of wine, meat, food and drink, and some clean clothes. The best things for me were the clothes, but putting them on felt like the strangest thing in the world at first. After this, we had to decide what to do with our prisoners.

We brought them out of the cave, and I told them that I was the governor of the island. I told them that we had taken the ship back from their new captain. And I said that because they had behaved so badly they had to be punished. If they went back to England, they would be killed. But I told them that if they wanted, they could stay on the island. I explained that I was leaving the island with all my men.

The prisoners were very thankful, and agreed to stay on the island. I told the captain that I would stay one more night on the island, while he got the ship ready. That night, I told the prisoners my story. I showed them how to make bread and plant corn, and how to dry grapes. I showed them how to look after the goats, and gave them guns and gunpowder. And I told them to behave well towards the Spanish men when they arrived on the island.

At last it was time for me to go onto the ship. I took my goatskin hat, my umbrella, my parrot and the money I had found, and on the 19th of December 1686, I left the island. I had been there for twenty-eight years, two months and nineteen days.

14

I Come Back to Europe

I arrived back in England in June 1687, having been away for thirty-five years. It was a strange place to me. I went to Yorkshire and found that my parents were dead. My only living relatives were my two sisters and my brother's two children.

After a while, I decided to go to Lisbon. I needed some money, and I wanted to find out about my plantation in Brazil. When I arrived there, I was happy to find my good friend the Portuguese sea captain, who had saved me and Xury from the sea off the coast of Africa. He was very old and he did not know me at first. But when he saw that it was really me, Robinson Crusoe, he was very happy.

The captain told me that my plantation in Brazil had done very well. He told me that it was being well looked after for me. He said that he was sure it would be returned to me now that I had come back.

The captain and I wrote letters to the people who had been looking after my plantation. And a few months later, they wrote back to me, sending me the money my plantation had made. Suddenly I found that I was a very rich man. As well as the five thousand pounds that had been sent to me, I had a plantation in Brazil which was making one thousand pounds a year. I could not believe how lucky I was. I was so amazed that for a while I became very ill.

When I was feeling better, I began to organize my money. My good old captain had been so kind and honest with me that I arranged for him to have an amount of money from me every year for the rest of his life. I also wanted to thank the widow of my old friend the English captain, who had looked after some money for me while I was away. She was now very poor, so I sent her some money and promised to send her some more. I also sent some money to my two sisters.

I wrote to the people in Brazil who had looked after my plantation, thanking them for their honesty. And then I decided to go back to England. My only problem now was that I could not decide how to get there. Strangely, I did not want to go by sea. Many bad things had happened to me at sea, but this was not the only reason. I had a bad feeling about going back to England by ship, and I changed my plans two or three times. And I was right to have a bad feeling. One of the ships I nearly went in was captured, and another was wrecked.

At last I decided to go by land to England. Five other people came with me, as well as Friday, and some servants. We had many adventures. When we tried to cross from Spain into France, there was so much snow that the roads were all closed. We had to go over the mountains instead. It was very cold, and because of the snow, lots of wolves[96] were coming down from the mountains looking for food. They killed any people or animals they found.

We came to one place where we had been told there were many wolves. As we were going across some open land with woods all around we suddenly saw about a hundred wolves coming towards us. We shot at them and then shouted at them, and at last they went away. But a little further on we heard more wolves in the woods, and then saw the bodies of a dead horse and two dead men, who had been eaten up by them. As we came close to the wood, we found that there were wolves all around us. There must have been three hundred of them.

They kept running towards us, and although we shot at them, they kept coming back. Then I told one of the servants to put a long line of gunpowder on some fallen trees, and set fire to it.

Some of the wolves fell in the fire, and the others moved back, and at last we were able to go forward. We were told later

Some of the wolves fell in the fire, and the others moved back.

that we were very lucky we had not been eaten by the wolves in those woods.

When I arrived back in England I decided to sell my plantation in Brazil. I brought my brother's two sons to live with me and I looked after them. The eldest lived as a gentleman[97], and the youngest became the captain of a ship. I got married myself, and had two sons and a daughter. But then my wife died, and I decided to go with my nephew in his ship to the East Indies.

We left in 1694, and on this voyage, I visited my old island. I found that after fighting with the prisoners, the Spanish men had now taken over the island. Everyone had to listen to them and do what they told them. Some of them had been to the mainland and brought back prisoners, including some women, so there were now about twenty young children there.

I stayed on my island for about twenty days, and left the people guns, gunpowder, clothes and tools, as well as two workmen – a woodworker and a metalworker – to help them. I then divided my island up into parts and gave the men different parts, although the island as a whole was still mine. When I got to Brazil I sent a boat back to the island, carrying more people, including seven women, and some cows and sheep.

After this, many more things happened on the island. Three hundred men came from the mainland and dug up the islanders' crops. The islanders fought with them, but lost, and three of them were killed. But later they fought with them once more and took the island again. All of these things, and some other very surprising things that happened to me, I may perhaps write about one day.

Points for Understanding

1

1 How were the men rescued from the ship on Robinson Crusoe's first voyage?
2 Why was the captain of the ship angry with Robinson Crusoe?

2

1 How did Robinson Crusoe make money on his first voyage to Africa?
2 What happened to him on his second voyage to Africa?
3 Why did the pirate captain let Robinson Crusoe go out in his boat?
4 How were Robinson Crusoe and Xury rescued?

3

1 What did Robinson Crusoe do in Brazil?
2 Why did he and the other planters and merchants decide to go to Africa?
3 What two things were they afraid of when their ship was blown away from the other merchant ships?
4 What happened to their ship?

4

1 Why was Robinson Crusoe so sad when he saw the ship near the shore?
2 Why did Robinson Crusoe go back to the ship?
3 How did he carry the things back from the ship?
4 Why did he want to build his hut near the sea?
5 How did he get into and out of his hut?
6 Why did he put up a piece of wood and make marks on it?

5

1 Why was there corn and rice growing near the hut?
2 Why did Robinson Crusoe decide to start reading the Bible?

6

1 What fruit did Robinson Crusoe find when he explored the island?
2 Why did he build a second home?
3 When did he learn was the best time to plant rice and corn?
4 What did he bring home from his trip to the other side of the island?

7

1 What things did Robinson Crusoe need to make his own bread?
2 Why did he make a canoe?
3 Why couldn't he use the canoe?
4 What happened to him when he tried to sail around the island?
5 How did he get back to shore?

8

1 Why did Robinson Crusoe decide to keep tame goats?
2 What did he see one day which made him very frightened?
3 What two things did he do to make himself safe?
4 How did he know that cannibals had come to his island?

9

1 What did Robinson Crusoe keep in the cave that he found?
2 What happened that made him want to escape from the island?
3 What idea did he get from his dream?
4 How did Robinson Crusoe save one of the cannibals' prisoners?
5 How did the prisoner show Robinson Crusoe that he wanted to be his slave?

10

1 Why did Robinson Crusoe call the prisoner Friday?
2 Why did Robinson Crusoe become angry with Friday?

11

1 Why didn't Friday want Robinson Crusoe to send him back to his country?
2 Why did Robinson Crusoe decide that he had to kill the cannibals when he saw them?
3 Why was Friday so excited when he saw the man in the boat?

12

1 Why did Robinson Crusoe feel like a king?
2 Why did Robinson Crusoe want the Spanish men to come to his island?
3 Why did the Spanish man and Friday's father go away?
4 Who did Friday think was coming when he saw the English boat?
5 How did Robinson Crusoe know that something was wrong when he saw the English boat come in?
6 What had happened on the English ship?
7 How did Robinson Crusoe help the captain?

13

1 Why did more men come out in a boat from the ship?
2 How did Robinson Crusoe stop them from going back to the ship?
3 What did the captain do to show Robinson Crusoe he had recaptured his ship?
4 Why did the prisoners decide to stay on the island?

14

1 Who did Robinson Crusoe give money to when he received the money from his plantation?
2 How did he travel from Portugal back to England?
3 How did he nearly die on the journey?
4 Who were the most important people on the island when Robinson Crusoe went back to visit?

Glossary

1 **candle** (page 4)
a stick of wax with a piece of string in it that you burn to give light.
2 **religious** (page 4)
relating to *religion* – belief in a god or gods – or a particular system of beliefs in a god or gods.
3 **get rid of** (page 4)
to do something so that you stop being affected by someone or something that is annoying or unpleasant.
4 **forgiven** – *to forgive someone* (page 4)
to decide to stop being angry with someone who has done something that is bad.
5 **spy** (page 4)
someone whose job is to find out secret information about a country or an organization.
6 **buried** – *to bury someone* (page 4)
to put someone's dead body in the ground during a funeral ceremony.
7 **set up** (page 5)
to start something such as a business, organization, or institution.
8 **plantation** (page 5)
a large farm where crops such as tea, coffee, cotton, and sugar are grown.
9 **tobacco** (page 5)
a type of leaf that people smoke in cigarettes.
10 **slave** (page 5)
someone who belongs by law to another person and who has to obey them and work for them.
11 **wrecked** (page 5)
destroyed or damaged very badly. Someone whose ship is badly damaged or destroyed is *shipwrecked*.
12 **voyage** (page 8)
a long journey, usually on a ship.
13 **rough** (page 8)
with a surface that is not smooth because of bad weather.
14 **seasick** (page 8)
feeling ill from the movement of the boat that you are travelling on.

15 *calmer* – *calm* (page 8)
calm water does not move very much.
16 *rum* (page 8)
a strong alcoholic drink.
17 *shore* (page 8)
the land that is on the edge of a sea or lake.
18 *wave* (page 8)
a line of water that rises up on the surface of a sea, lake, or river.
19 *fear* (page 9)
the feeling that you have when you think something bad is going to happen.
20 *prayed* – *to pray* (page 9)
to speak to God or a saint, for example to give thanks or to ask for help.
21 *leak* (page 9)
a hole or crack in something that a liquid or gas comes out of.
22 *sink* (page 9)
to disappear below the surface of water.
23 *captain* (page 9)
the person who is in charge of a ship or aircraft.
24 *fire* (page 9)
if a weapon fires, or if someone fires it, someone uses it to shoot something.
25 *die down* (page 9)
if something dies down, it becomes much less noisy, powerful, or active.
26 *rowed* – *to row* (page 9)
to move a boat through water using poles with flat ends called *oars*.
27 *pirate* (page 10)
someone who steals things from ships while they are sailing.
28 *widow* (page 11)
a woman whose husband has died.
29 *sail* (page 11)
a large piece of strong cloth fixed to a tall pole on a boat. It uses the wind to move the boat across water.
30 *shooting* – *to shoot* (page 13)
to hit someone or something with a bullet from a gun.
31 *gunpowder* (page 13)
a substance that is used for causing explosions and for firing weapons.
32 *drown* (page 13)
to disappear below the surface of water and die.

33 **master** (page 14)

a man who has control over servants, other people, or an animal.

34 **Christian** (page 15)

someone whose religion is Christianity.

35 **sand** (page 16)

a pale brown substance that you find at a beach or in the desert, formed from very small pieces of rock.

36 **breath** (page 17)

the air that goes in and out of your body when you breathe, or the action of getting air into your lungs. If you *take a breath*, you fill your lungs with air.

37 **knock me over/down** – *to knock someone over/down* (page 17)

to hit someone very hard, so that they fall.

38 **raft** (page 19)

a simple flat boat made by tying long pieces of wood together.

39 **tool** (page 19)

a piece of equipment that you hold to do a particular type of work.

40 **barrel** (page 19)

a large round container with a flat top and bottom, used for storing liquids and other substances.

41 **mainland** (page 19)

a large area of land that forms the main part of a country but does not include any islands.

42 **hut** (page 20)

a small simple building.

43 **tent** (page 20)

a structure made of cloth and supported with poles and ropes. You sleep in it when you are camping.

44 **Bible** (page 20)

the holy book of the Christian and Jewish religions.

45 **iron** (page 20)

a hard heavy metal that is used for making steel.

46 **shade** (page 21)

a slightly cool dark place where the light and heat from the sun does not reach.

47 **steep** (page 21)

a steep slope goes up or down very quickly.

48 **cave** (page 21)

a large hole in the side of a hill or under the ground.

49 *fence* (page 21)
    a flat upright structure made of wood or wire that surrounds an area
    of land.
50 **ladder** (page 21)
    a piece of equipment for reaching high places that consists of two
    long pieces of wood or metal joined by smaller bars where you put
    your feet when you climb.
51 **dug out** – *to dig something out* (page 21)
    to make a hole in the earth bigger by removing more earth.
52 **goat** (page 21)
    an animal similar to a sheep but with longer legs and a thinner coat.
53 **amazed** (page 24)
    very surprised.
54 **corn** (page 24)
    wheat, or any similar plant with seeds used for food.
55 **rice** (page 24)
    a food consisting of small white or brown seeds that are eaten
    cooked.
56 **earthquake** (page 24)
    a sudden shaking movement of the ground.
57 **shook** – *to shake* (page 24)
    to make lots of quick small movements up and down, or from side
    to side.
58 **turtle** (page 25)
    an animal with a shell and four short legs that lives mainly in water.
59 **fever** (page 25)
    a medical condition in which the temperature of your body is very
    high.
60 **explore** (page 26)
    to travel around an area in order to learn about it, or in order to
    search for something.
61 **lime** (page 26)
    a fruit with a hard green skin and sour juice.
62 **bower** (page 27)
    a pleasant place in a forest or garden where the trees protect you
    from the sun.
63 **parrot** (page 29)
    a brightly coloured tropical bird that is often kept as a pet and can
    be taught to copy what people say.

64 *canoe* (page 30)

a light narrow boat that you push through the water using a short pole with a flat end.

65 **crop** (page 30)

an amount of a plant that is grown for food.

66 **spade** (page 30)

a tool used for digging that consists of a handle and a flat part that you push into the earth.

67 **hedge** (page 30)

a line of bushes or small trees that grow close together around a garden or a field.

68 **grinding** – *to grind something* (page 30)

to break something into very small pieces or powder, either by using a machine or by crushing it between two hard surfaces.

69 **hunting** – *to hunt* (page 31)

to catch and kill animals to eat.

70 **oven** (page 31)

a piece of equipment that you cook food in.

71 **current** (page 32)

a strong movement of water or air in one direction.

72 **basket** (page 34)

a container for carrying or keeping things in, made from thin pieces of plastic, wire, or wood woven together.

73 **tame** (page 34)

to teach an animal not to be afraid of people or attack. An animal that has been tamed is described as *tame*.

74 **moustache** (page 34)

hair that grows above a man's mouth.

75 **footprint** (page 35)

a mark made by a human in a soft surface such as earth, snow, or sand.

76 **bone** (page 37)

one of the hard parts that form the frame inside your body.

77 **punish** (page 38)

to do something unpleasant to someone because they have done something bad or illegal.

78 **smoke** (page 38)

a grey, black, or white cloud that is produced by something that is burning.

79 **led** – *to lead somewhere* (page 38)
   if something such as a road, river, or door leads somewhere, or if it
   leads you there, it goes there.

80 **servant** (page 40)
   someone whose job is to cook, clean, or do other work in someone
   else's home.

81 **prisoner** (page 41)
   someone who has been caught by someone else and is not allowed
   to leave.

82 **bow and arrow** (page 41)
   a *bow* is a weapon made from a curved piece of wood. It is used for
   shooting *arrows* – thin straight sticks with a sharp point at one end
   and feathers at the other.

83 **kneeling down** – *to kneel down* (page 41)
   to put your knee or both knees on the ground.

84 **sword** (page 43)
   a weapon with a short handle and a long sharp blade.

85 **sign** (page 43)
   a movement or sound that you make in order to tell someone
   something.

86 **flesh** (page 45)
   the soft substance under your skin that consists mostly of muscle
   and fat.

87 **mast** (page 48)
   a tall pole that the sails hang from on a ship or boat.

88 **tied up** – *to tie someone up* (page 49)
   to tie a rope etc tightly around someone so that they cannot move
   or escape.

89 **weak** (page 50)
   lacking physical strength or good health.

90 **rubbed** – *to rub something* (page 52)
   to move your hands or an object over a surface firmly.

91 **mutiny** (page 52)
   an occasion when people refuse to obey someone in a position of
   authority.

92 **thunder and lightning** (page 53)
   thunder is the loud noise that you sometimes hear in the sky during
   a storm. *Lightning* is the bright flashes of light that you see during a
   storm.

93 **mate** (page 55)

someone whose job is to help the captain on a ship.

94 **passenger** (page 55)

someone who travels in a vehicle, aircraft, train, or ship but is not the driver or one of the people who works on it.

95 **governor** (page 60)

someone who is in charge of an area.

96 **wolves** – *wolf* (page 64)

a wild animal that looks like a large dog.

97 **gentleman** (page 66)

an old word for a man from a family in a high social class.

Exercises

Background

Choose the correct information to complete the sentences. The first one is an example.

1 The author of *Robinson Crusoe*, Daniel Defoe, was (English) / American.

2 He <u>came</u> / did not come from a rich family.

3 Defoe trained to be <u>an army officer</u> / <u>a minister of the church</u>.

4 He worked first as a <u>merchant</u> / <u>writer</u>.

5 After he got married he <u>became</u> / <u>did not become</u> a rich man.

6 He <u>liked</u> / <u>disliked</u> the King of England, James II.

7 He went to prison <u>once</u> / <u>twice</u> in his lifetime.

8 *Robinson Crusoe* was published <u>early</u> / <u>late</u> in Defoe's life.

9 *Robinson Crusoe* <u>was</u> / <u>was not</u> Defoe's only novel.

10 Defoe is buried <u>in Britain</u> / <u>abroad</u>.

Multiple choice

Tick the best answer. The first one is done for you.

1 Which island is the island in the novel probably based on?
   a Hawaii.
   b Tobago. ✓
   c Cuba.
   d Jamaica.

2 What did Robinson's father warn would happen if he went to sea?
   a He would be captured by pirates and killed.
   b He would never see his older brother again.
   c God would not be happy with him and no one would help him.
   d He would not be rich and his family would not give him money.

78

3 Why did Robinson let the captain of the Portuguese ship have the slave boy Xury?

   a Because the captain paid him much more than the normal price.

   b Because the captain promised to set Xury free in the future if he changed religion.

   c Because the captain had a gun and Robinson was afraid he would kill him if not.

   d Because Xury had to return to Europe.

4 Which of these did Robinson NOT take from the wreck when he found himself alone on the island?

   a Some cats and a dog.

   b A parrot.

   c Some money.

   d Some pieces of iron and wood.

5 Why did the roof of Robinson's cave fall in?

   a Because it had not been built with good tools.

   b Because cannibals attacked it.

   c Because there was an earthquake.

   d Because there was heavy rain.

6 Which of the following did NOT happen when Robinson was ill with a fever?

   a He took a medicine of tobacco and rum.

   b He had a frightening dream.

   c He started reading the Bible.

   d He was looked after by Friday.

7 Why did Robinson decide not to move his main home to the woodland area of the island?

   a Because he wanted a seaside home in case a ship passed.

   b Because he could not grow rice and wheat in the fruit-growing area.

   c Because he had worked hard on his hut and did not want to leave it.

   d Because it was too far to take his tools to build a new hut.

8 What was Robinson worried that he did not have enough of on the island?

   a Bread.

   b Wood.

   c Money.

   d Gunpowder.

9 Whose is the first man's voice that Robinson hears on the island?

   a Friday's.

   b A Spanish prisoner's.

   c An English captain's.

   d Poll's.

10 Which of the following did Robinson NOT teach Friday?

   a To make bread.

   b About the Christian religion and God.

   c About the people who lived in the land opposite, Trinidad.

   d How to make a fence.

11 What did the Spanish man have to promise before leaving the island with Friday's father?

   a That the Spanish men he returned with would do what Robinson said.

   b That the Spanish would never return to the island.

   c That they would be careful of the strong currents between the island and the mainland.

   d That they would teach Christianity to the people on the mainland.

12 Where did Robinson go first when he left the island?

   a Back to England.

   b Back to Brazil.

   c To Trinidad.

   d To Portugal.

Vocabulary: opposites in context

Choose the best OPPOSITE (a–d) of the underlined word from the story. The first one is done for you.

1. 'I also kept two or three <u>tame</u> cats' (p38)
   - **a** friendly   (**b** wild)   **c** fat   **d** different

2. 'Everyone knew that the ship was going to <u>sink</u>' (p9)
   - **a** go down   **b** fly   **c** float   **d** drown

3. 'So I took a gun, and climbed to the <u>top</u> of a small hill' (p19)
   - **a** peak   **b** centre   **c** under   **d** bottom

4. 'A terrible storm <u>blew up</u>' (p8)
   - **a** blew down   **b** died down   **c** went round   **d** stormed over

5. 'If I saw a ship, I could <u>light</u> a fire' (p21)
   - **a** light down   **b** put out   **c** start   **d** put over

6. 'On a <u>cloudy</u> day, I would not have been able to find my way back' (p33)
   - **a** overcast   **b** sunshine   **c** clear   **d** stormy

7. 'A <u>huge</u> wave hit our boat' (p17)
   - **a** thin   **b** dry   **c** big   **d** small

8. 'The sea was very <u>rough</u>' (p8)
   - **a** calm   **b** clear   **c** peace   **d** clean

9. 'He made lots of signs to show me how <u>thankful</u> he was' (p44)
   - **a** ungrateful   **b** unsurprised   **c** pleased   **d** unhappy

10. 'I wanted to find a place that had fresh water and <u>shade</u>' (p21)
    - **a** sunny   **b** darkness   **c** sun   **d** bright

Time expressions

Complete the sentences with a time expression from the box. You can use the words more than once. The first one is done for you.

| in | on | while | for | after | since | during | at | before |

1 Robinson Crusoe lived on the island ......_for_........ 28 years.

2 The captain agreed to set Xury free .... ten years time.

3 Robinson Crusoe was born .... 1632.

4 Robinson sailed to Africa .... the 1st September 1659.

5 A few months .... Robinson had arrived on the island, he found some corn growing.

6 Robinson thought that the turtle was the best food he had eaten .... arriving on the island.

7 .... his stay on the island, Robinson built many things including a hut and a canoe.

8 Once, just .... Robinson had stopped working on his hut, the roof caved in.

9 Robinson finally got back to England .... June 1687.

10 .... he was in Lisbon, Robinson met the Portuguese captain again.

11 The men had been away .... eight days when the English ship arrived on the island.

12 Robinson's servant got his name because Robinson had saved his life .... this day.

13 .... last Robinson had a good place on the island to make his home.

14 .... he left Brazil to go to Africa, Robinson found some people to look after his plantation.

Vocabulary: sea travel

Change the order of the letters in brackets to make words connected to sea travel. All of the words are in the story. The first one is an example.

1 Robinson's parents were not happy when he said he wanted to go on a sea ......*voyage*....... (GVOAYE).

2 When the sea was .... Robinson felt seasick (GOHRU).

3 During the hurricane, the sea .... (SWVAE) were so high that Robinson and the others were worried they would .... (WNODR).

4 During his second trip, Robinson's ship was travelling just off the .... (SOCTA) of Africa when they were captured by .... (SPERTIA).

5 Because of the leak in the ship, water started coming in and the ship started to .... (KISN).

6 The .... (PCAINTA) of the English ship had lost control when the other men on the ship started a .... (YMUITN).

7 Robinson made a .... (AFTR) from pieces of wood to help him carry things from the ship to the island.

8 In his third year, Robinson made his own .... (NCOEA) from wood to try to sail to the land, but it was too heavy.

9 When he was trying to sail around the island, the strong .... (RRECUTN) almost pulled him out to sea. Fortunately, he managed to get back to the .... (RSOHE), helped by the wind.

10 The sailors .... (WROED) away from their ship in a smaller boat.

11 Friday built a .... (STMA) for their boat while Robinson made a .... (LSAI).

Sentence transformations: *ask/tell somebody (not) to…*

In reported speech, we use 'ask' to report a request or question and 'tell' to report an order or command.

Change the direct speech sentences below into reported speech using *ask/tell* + object *(not)* + *to….* Write as if you are Robinson Crusoe (I/me). The first one is an example.

1 My father said to me, 'Stay at home and get a good job'.
   My father *told me to stay at home and get a good job.*

2 My father said to me, 'Don't go to sea'.
   My father

3 'Will you free the boy in ten years time?' I said to the captain.
   I

4 'Can you talk to my father?' I said to my mother.
   I

5 'Please take me back into the boat,' said Moley to me.
   Moley

6 'Call me master,' I said to the boy.
   I

7 'Please don't hurt me,' said Moley to me.
   Moley

8 I said to Friday, 'Do not dig the men up and eat them'.
   I

Grammar: *as* + adjective + *as...*

Choose the best expression from the box to complete each sentence. The first one is done for you.

> ~~as high as~~   as rich as   as fast as   as many as
>
> as far away as   as often as   as lonely as   as secret as

1   During the storm, the waves were ...... *as high as* ...... mountains.

2   After being pushed into the sea, Moley swam .... he could towards the boat.

3   When escaping from the pirates, Robinson tried to get .... possible from their ship.

4   With Friday as his servant, Robinson did not feel .... he had when he first arrived on the island.

5   Robinson built walls and planted trees to make his hut .... possible so that cannibals would not find it.

6   Robinson needed lots of goats in his enclosures for food, so he tamed .... possible.

7   Robinson was making some money from his sugar plantation but it was not enough for him. He wanted to become .... he could.

8   Robinson visited the woodland area of the island .... he could to collect grapes.

Double comparatives

Double comparatives are formed by repeating the comparative and joining them with *and*:

'I suddenly felt a little wind blowing up. It grew <u>stronger and stronger</u>' (p33)

Using the example above and in question 1, complete the sentences below using a double comparative form of an adjective from the box.

| rough | tired | heavy | rich | ~~dangerous~~ | safe | terrified | lucky |

1 As the weather got worse, the voyage got _..more and more dangerous.._ .

2 During the storm, the sea got ....

3 As Robinson built higher walls around his hut, he felt
   ....

4 As Robinson lay awake thinking about the huge footprint in the sand,
   he felt ....

5 As Robinson realised he had been saved when the others had died, he
   felt ....

6 As Friday made the men run all around the island, they got
   ....

7 Robinson became .... from his
   successful sugar plantation.

8 As the rains got ...., Robinson
   spent more time in his cave.

Making questions

Write questions for the answers.

> **Example:** *Who wrote Robinson Crusoe?*
> Daniel Defoe wrote *Robinson Crusoe*.

Q1 *Whose*

A1 Robinson Crusoe's older brother had been killed as a soldier.

Q2 *Why*

A2 Robinson went on the voyage to Africa to get slaves for his plantation.

Q3 *How*

A3 Only one person was alive after the ship was wrecked.

Q4 *How*

A4 Robinson travelled between the wreck and the island by raft.

Q5 *Which*

A5 He found grapes, melons, oranges and lemons in the woodland area.

Q6 *Who*

A6 Robinson saved Friday from the cannibals.

Q7 *How*

A7 Robinson spent 28 years on the island.

Q8 *Were*

A8 No, his parents were dead when he returned to England.

Macmillan Education
Between Towns Road, Oxford OX4 3PP
A division of Macmillan Publishers Limited
Companies and representatives throughout the world

ISBN 978–0–2307–3118–9
ISBN 978–0–2307–1656–8 (with CD pack)

This version of *Robinson Crusoe* by Daniel Defoe was retold by
Salma Gabol for Macmillan Readers.

First published 2009
Text © Macmillan Publishers Limited 2009
Design and illustration © Macmillan Publishers Limited 2009
This version first published 2009.

Illustrated by John Dillow and Peter Harper
Cover photograph by Punchstock/Photographer's Choice

Printed and bound in Thaila~ ·

2015   2014   201·
10   9   8   ¯

with C
2015   ∠∪14
11 10   9   8   7